Albino Luís Nunes Viveiros

Heritage, socio-cultural animation and local community development

Albino Luís Nunes Viveiros

Heritage, socio-cultural animation and local community development

A reading from the perspective of the socio-cultural animator

ScienciaScripts

Imprint
Any brand names and product names mentioned in this book are subject to trademark, brand or patent protection and are trademarks or registered trademarks of their respective holders. The use of brand names, product names, common names, trade names, product descriptions etc. even without a particular marking in this work is in no way to be construed to mean that such names may be regarded as unrestricted in respect of trademark and brand protection legislation and could thus be used by anyone.

Cover image: www.ingimage.com

This book is a translation from the original published under ISBN 978-613-9-72711-7.

Publisher:
Sciencia Scripts
is a trademark of
Dodo Books Indian Ocean Ltd. and OmniScriptum S.R.L publishing group

120 High Road, East Finchley, London, N2 9ED, United Kingdom
Str. Armeneasca 28/1, office 1, Chisinau MD-2012, Republic of Moldova, Europe
Printed at: see last page
ISBN: 978-620-7-75189-1

Index

Previous note

The essay that the reader has in hand is supported by the text of the communication *Heritage narratives and the trails of local community development: a revisitation from the perspective of the sociocultural animator* presented at the XXIV International Congress of Sociocultural Animation: Heritage and Community, in October 2017, in the city of Setúbal.

Based on the revised and expanded base text, we seek to discuss in a reflective manner peripheral themes and, simultaneously, areas of intervention that intersect with cultural heritage. It is our purpose to deepen the discussion around themes that cannot be "neglected", because they are central themes and add value to the public debate around heritage and local community development.

Heritage - cultural, natural, landscape, urban, recreational, musical, religious, ethnographic, archaeological, underwater, digital, military, architectural, vernacular, industrial, artistic and gastronomic - in their material and immaterial matrices are cultural assets of the local community with economic, educational and sociocultural value that should be enhanced from a local community development perspective.

Our conceptual vision of cultural heritage is based on a global perspective. When referencing the term heritage, we do so always considering the aggregation of adjectival plurality and the material and immaterial matrices.

Heritage as endogenous resources materializes in fragments of history and collective experiences, they are integral elements of the cultural, humanized and natural landscapes of rural and urban territories. Heritage as endogenous cultural assets are excellent means of mobilization for social, economic, cultural and educational development. One of the biggest challenges lies in raising awareness among groups and communities to exercise cultural citizenship in an (in)direct relationship with heritage education and animation.

The preservation and enhancement of heritage presupposes the design of a safeguard plan that involves the community in the process, based on heritage and tourism education programs, as this is a potential starting point for other sociocultural intervention projects in boosting and endogenous development of territories and local communities.

Local development is synonymous with integrated development. This paradigm points to the principle of community participation and the use of its assets, including heritage. From our perspective, local community development materializes from the intersection of educational, social, cultural and political spheres. Sociocultural animation can contribute to leveraging local community (development), considering the social equation “involve to develop”.

Local community development involves two possible driving elements: tourism and the social economy. In this analysis framework and within the scope of tourism as an instrument that enhances the safeguarding and valorization of heritage, it is legitimate to consider the contribution of tourist activity and the social economy to the development of the community. A development paradigm architected in the methodology and principles of sociocultural animation.

1. The conceptualizations of heritage in international and national regulations

The social projection of heritage contributes to the maintenance of community dynamics, to the transmission of traditional knowledge and practices in a logic of “living culture”, the affirmation of cultural identity, social cohesion and job creation. Heritage as a collective heritage is recognized with socio-cultural values - identity, authenticity, diversity and integrity -, an educational dimension and socio-economic profitability arising from its safeguarding and social enjoyment.

In this path of ideas, we believe that it is important to clarify the principles and meanings attached to heritage. The reflection on a selected set of recommendations and conventions from international organizations on heritage is based on the principle evoked by the Council of the European Union (2014a): «[...] cultural heritage is a common resource and a common good and that caring for the Heritage is, therefore, a common responsibility.” (p. 1).

The *Convention for the Protection of World Cultural and Natural Heritage* (United Nations Educational, Scientific and Cultural Organization [UNESCO], 1972) approved by Portugal in 1979 (Decree no. 49/79, of 6 July), considers *monuments* as architectural, sculptural works or monumental paintings, among other heritage elements with exceptional value from the point of view of history, art or science, as cultural heritage. This conceptual framework includes *sets* described as groups of buildings that, due to their architecture or landscape integration, have relevant value. The United Nations Educational, Scientific and Cultural Organization (UNESCO) also considers, as references to cultural heritage, *places of interest* described as works resulting from human action or combined between human action and nature; Included are sites of archaeological interest with exceptional universal value from a historical, aesthetic, ethnological or anthropological point of view.

Within the scope of the *Convention for the Protection of World Cultural and*

Natural Heritage, natural heritage is considered to be *natural monuments* made up of physical and biological formations, or groups of these same formations; geological and *physiographic formations* and *strictly delimited areas* constituting the habitat of threatened fauna and flora species; *natural places of interest* or *closely delimited natural areas.* These heritage assets have in common the exceptional universal value from the perspective of aesthetics, science, conservation and natural beauty.

The concept of *historic complex* in light of the *Recommendation on the safeguarding of historic complexes and their function in contemporary life* (UNESCO, 1976) is defined as the group of buildings and spaces that constitute a human settlement in urban or rural areas - pre-historic sites. historic cities, old neighborhoods, villages and houses, monumental and homogeneous ensembles preserved without alteration - whose cohesion and value are recognized from the perspective of archaeological, architectural, prehistoric, aesthetic or sociocultural interest (UNESCO, 1976, p. two).

UNESCO states that historical complexes and their context in the natural and humanized environment constitute *per se* "[...] an irreplaceable universal heritage." (UNESCO, 1976, p. 3) and emphasizes that safeguard plans - identification, protection, conservation, restoration, rehabilitation, maintenance and revitalization - of historic complexes and their surroundings must include the maintenance of commerce, traditional activities and the development of harmonized cultural activities. The involvement of local populations in the safeguarding process is considered a principle of participation, because the dimension of human activities is an integral element of historical ensembles.

From our perspective, it is important to highlight UNESCO's call for attention to the urgent adoption of a policy for the protection and (re)animation of historical sites and their framing in the context of local, regional and national development.

Safeguard plans must include «[...] studies of social, economic, cultural and technical structures, [...]» and «[...] an analysis of economic, social and cultural activities, the way of life and social relations, [...]." (UNESCO, 1976, p. 5). On the other hand, safeguarding should stimulate the cohesion of the social fabric, the active maintenance of accommodation, commercial spaces and their workshops, lifestyle, traditional occupations, the revitalization of the training of artisans and "specialists in safeguarding complexes historical» and the development of crafts.

The *Vienna Declaration* (European Forum of Those Responsible for Heritage [FERP], 2009) highlights the importance of adopting investment policies in heritage. This asset contributes to sustainable economic recovery and is found «[...] within communities, stimulating social cohesion, as well as a sense of identity and belonging to a place.» (FERP, 2009, p. 1).

Investment in heritage has positive repercussions in three strategic dimensions for community sustainability: economic, resulting in the growth of cultural tourism and long-term economic and social benefits; environmental with the recovery of historic buildings, thus minimizing negative impacts on urban and rural fabrics; and sociocultural, because history and heritage sustain local, regional and national identities.

The International Council on Monuments and Sites (ICOMOS), through the latitude and longitude of its conception of heritage, encompasses natural and cultural landscapes (landscapes, historic sites and locations, built environments, past and continuing cultural practices, biodiversity, collections, knowledge and lived experiences). Heritage is the living record of the «[...] long process of historical development, forming the essence of diverse national, regional, indigenous and local identities and is an integral part of modern life.». Heritage is a «[...] dynamic point of reference and a positive instrument for development and exchange.» (International Council on Monuments and Sites [ICOMOS], 1999, p. 2).

ICOMOS (1999, p. 2) emphasizes that the heritage and collective memory of each place or community are irreplaceable and fundamental cultural assets for present and future sustainable development. This development model has the communication of the meanings of heritage, a key element that, from our perspective, goes beyond the vital process of conservation and socio-cultural enjoyment by the community. We talk about the paradigm of social and economic profitability in favor of local community development.

In terms of conceptual framework, it is important to consider the Portuguese legal system. Law No. 107/2001, of 8 September, states that elements of cultural heritage are material and immaterial assets that testify to civilizational or cultural values, bearers of relevant cultural interest, and must be the object of protection and valorization and that constitute structures of identity and collective memory. In the heritage context, the relevant cultural interest (historical, paleontological, archaeological, architectural, linguistic, documentary, artistic, ethnographic, scientific, social, industrial or technical) will reflect values of memory, antiquity, authenticity and uniqueness.

Intangible cultural heritage (UNESCO, 2003; Decree-Law no. 139/2009, of 15 June, republished by Decree-Law no. 149/2015, of 4 August) is understood as cultural manifestations embodied by practices, representations, expressions, objects, artefacts, cultural spaces associated with them, knowledge and skills of a traditional nature recognized by individuals, groups and communities as an integral part of their heritage and which are continually recreated depending on the environment, interaction with nature and history, projecting them a sense of collective memory and transmitted from generation to generation.

Heritage in its intangible matrix manifests itself in the domains of traditions and oral expressions; artistic expressions and manifestations of a performative nature; social practices, rituals and festive events; knowledge and practices related to nature and the universe; skills in the context of traditional processes and techniques.

National gastronomy is an integral element of the Portuguese intangible cultural heritage (Resolution of the Council of Ministers no. 96/2000, of 7 July), the result of traditional knowledge that imparts cultural value through regional diversity in enriching the national gastronomic recipe and economic value for tourist attractiveness, paving the way for a process of preserving its authenticity, valorization and dissemination to future generations.

National gastronomy as a traditional Portuguese recipe incorporates faunal and floristic elements used at local, regional and national levels; agri-food products of national origin that, due to their unique characteristics, reveal interest from a historical, ethnographic, social or technical point of view, highlighting values of memory, authenticity, antiquity and uniqueness.

The concept of heritage subscribed to by the *Framework Convention of the Council of Europe on the Value of Cultural Heritage for Society* (Resolution of the Assembly of the Republic no. 47/2008, of 18 July) summarizes social time and the matter of heritage. This community resource is defined as a set of assets inherited from the past and identified by people as a reflection and expression of their values, beliefs, knowledge and traditions in permanent evolution; it brings together aspects of the environment, the result of the interaction of communities and places throughout history.

The *Framework Convention* is committed to promoting a social and economic environment favorable to citizens' participation in public debate, safeguarding and initiatives relating to heritage, as well as its protection as an integral element of the objectives of sustainable development, cultural diversity and of contemporary creation. Reinforcing social cohesion and strengthening the dynamics of cultural, social, economic and political development through the use of heritage assets are commitments linked to the document.

2. Heritage and its social function: a proposal for clarification from the perspective of the sociocultural animator

Cultural heritage is the social representation of the community's culture and identity; It is its greatest asset because it generates social cohesion, fosters sociocultural dynamics, feeds back into community identity and drives local and regional economies. Cultural heritage has «[...] a public, community sense and broad collective identification.» (Pereiro Pérez, 2013, p. 163). Heritage is more than the "lever of memory". This cultural asset is a symbolic representation of culture (Pereiro Pérez, 2013, p. 163), it brings together all spiritual meanings and, at the same time, gains collective relevance (Miranda, 2011, p. 159).

Cultural assets are endogenous resources, carrying symbolic, social, economic, environmental and cultural values (Council of the European Union, 2014, p. 2) of civilizational significance and collective identity that could contribute to the revitalization of low-density and strengthening the social ties of groups and communities.

Cultural assets are characterized by «[...] valuable testimony to the civilization and culture they represent, [...] suitable for collective enjoyment,[...]» (Leitão, 2011, pp. 319-320), therefore, such enjoyment «[...] is legally recognized as a diffuse interest of the community [...].» (Leitão, 2011, p. 332), regardless of whether the assets are in the private, public or religious domain.

Regarding the principle of cultural enjoyment of heritage, Law no. 13/85, of 6 July, amended by Law no. 19/2000, of 10 August and Law no. 107/2001, of 8 of September, declares the principle of responsibility of the State, autonomous regions and local authorities in promoting mechanisms for raising awareness and participation of citizens in safeguarding cultural heritage, as a right and duty inherent to the exercise of citizenship, realization of the right to culture and to the enjoyment of cultural assets.

The principle of social equity in participation in cultural life is subject to the economic condition of the populations. This criterion is a piece of the political puzzle, as such, it must be considered in cultural development programs as a dimension of local community development.

The right to culture is a dimension of citizen participation in public life; the limitation or conditionality of participation channels makes access to culture and the enjoyment of cultural goods difficult.

Access to culture (UNESCO, 1976a, p. 152) is qualified by the real possibility of citizens, through the creation of economic conditions, to access information, training, knowledge and the free exercise of critical thinking and the enjoyment of values and goods cultural.

Cultural heritage for Pereiro Pérez (2013, p. 162) is the symbolic representation of groups, it is a community sign capable of generating and reinforcing identities, of promoting solidarity, of creating "social borders", of covering up internal differences and conflicts, of build community images. According to this author «[...] cultural heritage is an expression of the culture of human groups that recovers memories, ritualizes sociability, selects cultural assets and transmits legacies for the future.» (Pereiro Pérez, 2013, p. 164).

Heritage, in addition to the transmission of values, comprises several extensions: cultural, environmental, social, physical (spatial), economic, educational, scientific and digital (Council of Europe, 1975; Hernández Hernández, 2002; European Commission, 2004; Council of the European Union , 2014a). We understand that they are not just components, but lines of action to be considered in intervention programs and projects, whose human capital associated with the heritage legacy is an included element of heritage policies.

The valorization and dynamization of heritage through intervention projects mediated by sociocultural animators are a social commitment to the history, collective memory and culture of local communities. Heritage as cultural assets contributes to social integration and cohesion, to the sense of being a community (FERP, 2009, p. 1).

The conceptualization of heritage cannot be conditioned to a reductive vision, limited to an old building, or to a tradition forgotten in social time, on the contrary, thinking about heritage is talking about and intervening in surrounding areas, expanding the conceptual range to groups and sites which include historic centers, cultural landscapes as places and elements of traditional interest (Serrano, 2007, p. 8). The inclusive vision of Ribeiro Telles (personal communication, 2004) points to the non-separation between urban and rural landscapes. The landscape is the expression of the space lived by Man.

From our perspective, some principles and guidelines set out in the document *La Valletta Principles for the Safeguarding and Management of Historic Cities and Urban Complexes* (ICOMOS, 2011) summarize the global, plural and inclusive framework of the "social fabrication" of cultural heritage and its material and immaterial constituents, a line of thought open to social dynamics and passive guidance for the work of sociocultural animators within the scope of community intervention with direct reference to cultural assets.

Heritage has achieved a relevant social, cultural, educational, economic and political dimension in contemporary society. The relationship between cultural heritage and sustainable development is inseparable (Hernández Hernández, 2002). This is an aggregation of the sociocultural, environmental, economic and educational segments in an awakening of collective consciousness towards the social commitment to safeguarding cultural assets in a dynamic intrinsic to the community. It is essential that we talk about the spirit of the place as a set of tangible and intangible elements that invest the territory with identity and meanings. (ICOMOS, 2011, pp. 2-3).

In this analysis, it is essential to read about possible changes in the social and cultural environment of places, specifically, the suppression of traditional cultural activities, uses and practices, as signs of identity of the *modus operandi* and *modus vivendi* of the local community. The probable causes, among others, could be the aging of the population and human desertification, the mass touristization of territories, the fragility of social ties and, consequently , the fragmentation of rural and urban social fabrics.

Tourism can play a fundamental social role in local and regional socioeconomic dynamics, when promoted in harmony with the interests of the host community and with respect for the authenticity of cultural assets.

Governance is a vital socio-political segment in safeguarding heritage and sustainable development, because the exercise of active citizenship by interested parties reflects the cultural diversity of the territory. The safeguard plan must prioritize the authenticity, identity and integrity of places and communities, as civilizational values are created by culture.

In the global vision, it is pertinent to consider historical complexes and their spaces in rural and urban environments as a distinctive element, where human activities, buildings, spatial structure and surrounding areas are inserted, that is, the humanized landscape, because the Human activity is an integral element of the historical set (UNESCO, 1976, pp. 2-3).

In the *Recommendation relating to the participation and contribution of popular masses in cultural life* (UNESCO, 1976a), a series of measures are listed, including the safeguarding and rehabilitation of all forms of cultural expression; the reconciliation of heritage in its relationship with the past and contemporary times, in a contribution to the essential balance of societies and the creation of effective mechanisms for the active participation of citizens in public life, in particular, in the safeguarding of heritage.

It is in this conceptual, but complementary, diversity that sociocultural animators must view the heritage of the local community - an active aggregator of "living culture" and community identity -, with a strong index for the dynamization of the territory as a non-segregating heritage space, a space of inclusion and integration of communities and heritage, symbolic fusion of rural and urban territories, place of belonging and socialization of groups with different cultural, educational, political, social and economic portfolios.

3. Social participation in the agenda of public heritage policies

Citizens, through the exercise of active citizenship in the context of cultural rights, assume a role of individual and collective civic co-responsibility shared with public institutions, the business sector, non-governmental organizations and other associative structures in safeguarding heritage that can be monetized in favor of the development for the common good and its transmission to future generations.

Cultural governance according to the Council of the European Union (2012, p. 8, 2014) is not limited to a method of implementing cultural policies, including heritage policies. Governance is an instrument that facilitates greater integration of culture into the priorities of public policies through transversality with other sectoral policies - tourism, social cohesion and local development, education, urbanism, environment, economy, youth, among others - which can promote the principles of inclusion and sustainability, with a view to reinforcing the participatory involvement of the various local actors in the creation of strategies aimed at safeguarding heritage.

Heritage policies must be implemented transversally with other policies supported by structured dialogue forums with various civil society organizations, in particular, with heritage defense communities and informal groups of citizens with direct or indirect action on cultural assets. .

The appropriation of heritage as cultural assets, without losing its symbolic and civilizational values, is subject to social changes, political will expressed in cultural policies and economic variations in local, regional, national and European contexts.

Heritage must be safeguarded in the context of participatory governance. It is in this socio-political framework that the perspective of a *heritage community* set out in the *Framework Convention of the Council of Europe on the Value of Cultural Heritage for Society* (Resolution of the Assembly of the Republic no. 47/2008, of 18 July) and defined as a group of people who value certain elements of cultural heritage and who, through public initiative, intend to contribute to its sustainability and pass it on to future generations.

Within the framework of citizens' participation in the governance of cultural heritage, let us consider three basic categories in terms of cultural rights listed in the Constitution of the Portuguese Republic (Miranda, 2011, pp. 173-180): *rights referring to cultural identity* (right to cultural identity as component of the right to personal identity, the right to use language, the right to defend cultural heritage), *cultural freedoms* (cultural creation and enjoyment, dissemination of cultural works and access to cultural goods - means and instruments of cultural action and goods of the cultural heritage, cultural initiative -, among others) and the *right of access to cultural assets* (right to cultural enjoyment with extension to the right of access to cultural heritage).

From our perspective, the real implementation of cultural rights has its sociopolitical genesis in the context of the definition and implementation of a cultural policy based on directive actions that involve the political involvement of cultural organizations, cultural agents and actors, educational institutions and, not least important, in the exercise of cultural citizenship. By the way, Chaui (2006) points out two basic guidelines of cultural citizenship: culture as a right and as a work of creation. This idea takes us to the principles of active citizenship, which has citizens' participation as the main focus of cultural democracy.

The exercise of cultural rights is articulated with the process and dynamics of cultural activity, in communication between sociocultural actors and institutions, in the plural discussion of policies and in experimentation through cultural practices.

The binomial community and heritage is the subject of different social grammars, of interpretations in the light of various technical-scientific knowledge and of the construction of socio-political narratives that tend to leverage the principle of social participation through the participatory governance of cultural heritage (Council of the European Union, 2014a). This governance model is observed as an instrument that plays relevant social and political roles in the field of democratic participation, sustainability and social cohesion.

UNESCO (1976a, pp. 152-153) classifies the concept of participation in cultural life as the effective possibility of the group or individual to express, communicate, act and create freely with the purpose of guaranteeing their own development, a harmonious and the cultural progress of society. UNESCO associates different policies with participation in cultural life, including development and social progress, continuing education, environmental and communication policies.

The fundamentals added to the instruments for safeguarding heritage - identification, protection, preservation, restoration, rehabilitation, maintenance, revitalization and transmission - must be implemented at the local level of public policies, within the framework of cultural rights and, consequently, in the animation of heritage and the cultural identity of communities.

Citizen participation is a sign of public policies, to which heritage policies included in cultural policies (Ander-Egg, 1992; López de Aguileta, 2000) are no exception in terms of continuous promotion of the exercise of cultural citizenship and in the involvement of civil society organizations. In this domain there is a challenge to consider: the process of heritage awareness (UNESCO, 2003, p. 3) in the contexts of formal, informal and non-formal education, based on local and regional institutional networks, capable of implementing actions that are expected be boosted via sociocultural projects aimed at heritage education.

Cultural assets include structuring dimensions for citizens' lives. Heritage plays a socio-economic role of relevant community interest: social cohesion, promoting the creation of local jobs and reinforcing the feeling of community (European Commission, 2004), without neglecting the civic role through the community intervention that associations and citizens develop the safeguarding of heritage (UNESCO, 1976, 2003).

Participatory heritage governance must prioritize the cooperation of public authorities with the business sector and other civil organizations. At the local political-administrative level, municipal councils must appropriately exercise their duties and powers in terms of survey, classification, administration, maintenance, recovery and dissemination of the municipality's natural, cultural, landscape and urban heritage (Law no. 75/2013, of September 12th, amended by Rectification no. 46-C/2013, of November 1st and Rectification no. 50-A/2013, of November 11th, Law no. 25/2015, of March 30, Law No. 69/2015, of July 16, Law No. 7-A/2016, of March 30, Law No. 42/2016, of December 28 and Law No. 50 /2018, August 16), with direct responsibility for the authenticity of these cultural assets. The safeguarding process is responsible for stimulating sociocultural integration.

Regarding the pluralist vision of social participation, UNESCO (1976, p. 7) highlights the necessary communion of efforts representing the owners of heritage assets, inhabitants and users in a consultative capacity in the decision-making, management and animation bodies of construction projects. safeguard, or the creation of mixed economy organizations (social and solidarity economy) that participate in the implementation of policies.

ICOMOS (1999, p. 3), from a perspective of tourist sustainability based on heritage assets, also with an emphasis on collective social participation, highlights the necessary involvement and cooperation of local communities, tour operators, owners, authors of public policies and of site managers. This vision of sustainable tourist development is close to the position of Pereiro Pérez (2013, p. 182), when he conceptualizes development as a process of building " social futures", which involves practices, speeches and imaginaries that aim to achieve social change in a group, community or territory.

The premises of citizen participation in cultural governance, in particular, of heritage, are convergent. It is recognized that the right to heritage is inherent to the right to participate in cultural life. The aim of safeguarding heritage and its sustainable use is human development and the social well-being of local communities.

In this framework of usufruct, people have the right to the benefits of cultural assets and to contribute through the exercise of cultural citizenship to the enrichment of these assets in a harmonious economic and social environment

(Resolution of the Assembly of the Republic no. 47/2008, of 18 December July; Council of the European Union, 2014). This is a pressing challenge for sociocultural animators.

4. Raise awareness and dynamize: heritage education and sociocultural animation

Heritage education as an instrument of "cultural literacy" (Grunberg, Horta, & Monteiro, 1999) enables the reading of the territory and community dynamics, the understanding of the sociocultural universe and the social and historical times of society.

Heritage education goes beyond the school space. It is an education characterized as a non-formal and informal learning methodology (Duarte, 1994; Florêncio, 2012; Cuenca López, 2014; Pinto, 2014), among the objectives of heritage education are the interpretation, socialization and animation of heritage. Cultural assets as educational instruments can be worked on in the areas of formal, non-formal and informal education in the context of lifelong learning and training (UNESCO, 1976, p. 3, 2003; Council of the European Union, 2014a).

Heritage education is a teaching and learning process that has its primary source in cultural assets, generating new knowledge in a continuous process of cultural creation (Grunberg, *et al.,* 1999, p. 6). Cuenca López (2014, p. 80) defines heritage education as a discipline responsible for the analysis and development of didactic proposals of an investigative, interdisciplinary and socio-critical nature in which the design and development of purposes, contents and methodologies allow the construction of identity values, foster intercultural respect, social change and contribute to the formation of cultural citizenship. Heritage assets as objects of appreciation of the past empower actors through the appropriation and valorization of cultural assets.

Education for heritage must integrate the domain of public policies on culture and education with links to other sectoral policies, heritage and community spaces as places of non-formal and informal educational practices in a plan of involvement of educational, social and cultural agents, with the aim of ensuring processes that favor effective community participation.

It is within the scope of heritage education and the «interdependence and complementarity» (Duarte, 1994, p. 10) of triangulation - museum, school, community - and other historical-cultural places as spaces of culture, collective memory and community identity capable of development of sociocultural animation projects in which groups and communities will develop other learning and awareness skills to safeguard heritage as endogenous resources with potential for educational, tourist and economic development.

The interconnection between heritage education and the participation of citizens in cultural life, in particular, in heritage policies, signals the objective of heritage socialization that takes place through educational proposals, through which the connections between heritage and community through the exercise of active citizenship contribute for the cultural identity, training and training of local actors. Patrimonial socialization is a process that contributes to community development in a social, cultural, educational and economic sense (Cuenca López, 2014).

The *Asociación para la Interpretación del Patrimonio* (1999, p. 1) cited by Pereiro Pérez (2003, p. 249) argues that the interpretation of heritage «[...] is the art of revealing in situ the meaning of the natural and cultural to the public who visit these places in their leisure time.». The interpretation of heritage assets (Pereiro Pérez, 2003, pp. 251-252) is a method of presentation, communication and discovery that aims to appropriate and use these resources for cultural, educational, social and tourist purposes.

The interpretative process must be built based on the knowledge and experiences of citizens as a way of rooting in local identity. Interpretation makes it possible to create products and services based on safeguarding heritage and are linked to sustainable development processes.

In the context of heritage interpretation and animation, it seems important to mention the technique of "live history" (Coelho & Monteiro, 1987) as a cultural animation methodology developed in the context of historical recreation events and a larger project of dynamization, valorization and education for the historical-cultural heritage of local communities. "Live history" is an experience lived and participated by locals, in a privileged time-space for formal, non-formal and informal learning.

Historical recreation projects, teaching activities, workshops organized in museum spaces and other cultural dynamics recorded in heritage spaces using interactive experiences, dramatizations of historical scenes, thematic exhibitions, the promotion of traditional arts and crafts with the realization From live workshops, to artistic residencies, among other projects of an artistic nature, and tourist-cultural itineraries are important instruments for the involvement of local actors in the processes of valuing heritage.

The appreciation of heritage through cultural enjoyment contributes to the social construction of collective memory, to the affirmation of community identity before others and promotes local and regional economies.

In the context of heritage animation, it is plausible to refer to the environmental animation that results from nature tourism. In the context of tourist activity, heritage education actions that value traditional know-how and spaces for community socialization can be promoted, that is, a heritage education project integrated into a sustainable tourism development program.

In the context of environmental animation, animation activities, services and installations include projects or initiatives that integrate the following heritage assets: gastronomy; traditional products; traditional arts and crafts; thematic itineraries (religious, vernacular, military architecture); traditional social, educational and commercial establishments; fairs, festivals and pilgrimages; the thematic routes; traditional games; the entertainment hubs (place where entertainment events gather, which can integrate aspects of interpretation and nature sports) and traditional means of transport (Regulatory Decree no. 18/99, of 27 August, amended by Regulatory Decree no. .° 17/2003, of 10 October).

In Duarte's view (1994, p. 67), heritage education is a process of learning how to look, of choosing what to see, of discoveries and dialogue about heritage objects, memory spaces and people. It is in this relationship of seeing, feeling and cultural dialogue that intervention processes should be outlined, following the methodology of sociocultural animation through dynamics that involve cultural and educational institutions. Local authorities, cultural and recreational communities, the local business community and other civil society organizations are potential partners and “multipurpose entertainment spaces” (Duarte, 1994) in addition to schools and museums. One of the challenges lies in education as an instrument of heritage awareness (Hernández Hernández, 2002; Assunção, 2017).

Heritages are cultural assets of high importance as an instrument of local development. Sociocultural animators as development agents have the responsibility of interpreting cultural assets, as sociocultural and political constructions, the result of local *modus vivendi and support of community identity.* The social definition of heritage assets is the result of the community's social interaction in appropriating the territory as a common space for sociocultural connections.

The cultural dynamization of heritage resources implies a permanent process of social mediation and horizontal communication between citizens, the municipal government and local organizations committed to safeguarding heritage. This sociopolitical commitment involves dynamics that promote citizen participation, actions in response to the real needs of citizens and compliance with the collective interest.

It is due to the awareness process that people will be able to take positions for change in the face of the community's sociocultural reality. Freedom of thought and autonomy for action facilitate the participation of local actors in heritage education initiatives and the direction of cultural assets for sustainable tourism development.

In the context of cultural heritage management, Garrido Arroyo and Hernández Carretero (2014, p. 62) consider the management intervention of cultural heritage from the methodology of sociocultural animation, as they understand that this methodology contemplates the promotion of social participation and development of self-management. The authors argue that the heritage management process based on the teaching of participation promotes the use of resources and the appreciation of heritage from grassroots organizations and local agents themselves.

In our view, the exercise of cultural citizenship is an essential instrument for the animation of heritage, if not, the didactic sociocultural animation of participation and an instrument for community development. According to Garrido Arroyo and Hernández Carretero (2014, p. 62) there is a direct and influential relationship between sociocultural animation and citizen participation in actions in the field of cultural heritage management, with influence on citizens' commitment to the dynamics of heritage management.

UNESCO (1976, p. 7) highlights the importance of sociocultural animation activities linked to the safeguarding of built historical heritage and defends a line of intervention marked by the authenticity of social and cultural environments by recording the maintenance of existing functions as long as they are adequate and the creation of others, whose sustainability must be compatible with the social and economic contexts of the locality. The possible adaptability of the functions of the historic building must meet the social, cultural and economic needs of citizens.

UNESCO (1976, p. 7) considers that a cultural animation policy should contribute to the conversion of historical complexes into centers of cultural activities, with an essential role in the cultural development of communities.

The heritage valorization proposed by UNESCO, according to our reading, promotes historical dignification through the rehabilitation of built heritage and its conversion into sociocultural equipment, making them available to the local community as spaces for community socialization, to promote associations youth, for the development of sociocultural animation projects and, consequently, encouraging citizen participation in cultural life. We understand that this measure is part of the municipal cultural policy framework (Ander-Egg, 1992, p. 43; López de Aguileta, 2000, p. 96).

5. Sociocultural animation and local community development

Community development, local development or integrated development is a topic of multiple readings and spaces for intervention for technicians from different disciplinary areas, whose actions intersect in the processes of mediation and community intervention.

Community development strategies have structuring characteristics (Silva, 1994, p. 609): greater investment in processes to the detriment of intervention content, strong educational component, mobilization of endogenous social resources, option for long-term investments sustained more in local partnerships than than in the temporary intervention of technicians and animators external to the community.

In the approach to integrated development, Silva (1994, p. 612) highlights two fundamental links: one to the territory as «places-spaces» built and lived by Man; the other, to a community for its history, its culture, its groups and members. Integrated development are "globalizing strategies of local intervention" (Silva, 1994, p. 612) that seek integration between processes and appreciation of community cultures; processes that mobilize resources, social transformation and future change.

In this context, we understand that sociocultural animation as a social technology and educational methodology that promotes participation, integrates the dynamics of community development (Dias & Palma, 2001; Sanchéz Sanchéz, 2002) because participation facilitates awareness processes that emerge from educational and of sociocultural action, leverages the social transformation of ideas in projects aimed at community development.

Local development is the «process that mobilizes people and institutions seeking to transform the local economy and society» (Jesus, 2003 *apud* Silva & Silva, 2008, p. 5) by facilitating the creation of new employment opportunities, which leads to favoring the living conditions and well-being of the local community.

The Economic and Social Council considers that local development implies «[...], the leading role in projects by local authorities and local economic and social agents, [...].» (Economic and Social Council, 1996, p. 7). The involvement of political and social actors strengthens participatory democracy, generates synergies that enhance the use of endogenous resources, adds value to initiatives and enhances the community's social capital.

It is important to think about local development from the ground up, that is, development policies must be structured in the socio-cultural and economic realities of the territory. The community, local resources and civil society organizations are the vital support for the implementation of development policies, without forgetting that the local development model is not a unique format, as «[...] each local reality constitutes a microcosm endowed with specificities, which can follow its own development paths." (Economic and Social Committee of the European Communities *apud* Economic and Social Council, 1996, p. 21).

Local development refers to the location that, in a sociological sense, constitutes a community (Quintana Cabanas, 1995, p. 185). A community (Ander-Egg, 2003, p. 25) is a grouping of people who inhabit a delimited or delimitable geographic space, whose members are aware of belonging or identify with a local symbol, interacting with each other with more energy when compared with another context, they operate in communication and reciprocal support networks aimed at achieving specific objectives, satisfying needs, solving problems or performing relevant social functions at a local level.

The term community development applied in a narrow sense is appropriate to local development (Quintana Cabanas, 1995, p. 185). The local is the most appropriate environment for developing community development programs (Ander-Egg, 2003, p. 113).

Community development and local development from the perspective of Quintana Cabanas (1995, p. 185) are synonymous and community animation is an intervention methodology specific to community development. This author suggests a series of action proposals to promote local development in accordance with the socio-political, socio-cultural, socio-educational and socio-economic spheres. In socio-political terms, there is a need to encourage citizen participation in local initiatives. In sociocultural terms, it is vital to provide autonomy for groups to exercise the right to their own identity and difference, to provide information so that each person can decide autonomously, and the development of field work must be based on interdisciplinary teams. In socio-educational education, it is imperative to encourage ongoing training, encourage the formation of groups and encourage processes of community awareness-raising and consequent actions. In socio-economic terms, the focus is on promoting social and alternative economies (Quintana Cabanas, 1995, pp. 188-189).

Community animation is a scope of sociocultural animation when the emphasis is capitalized on the social (Lopes, 2006, p. 372). The social is structuring for local community development. From our perspective, there are no participatory processes and effective practices of community animation without the active involvement of local actors, the promotion of critical awareness and the driving autonomy of discernment about social and cultural realities.

The place is a space for multiple learning and the dissemination of community practices, it is a space for strengthening the feeling of belonging to a territory and a community, for the pulse of social, cultural and human values as a compliment to pluralism and freedom of civic action . Quintanas Cabanas (1995, p. 189) states that the philosophy of local development requires the search for citizen participation, the decentralization of initiatives and actions, the promotion of associations and the promotion of volunteering.

It is through the strengthening of the social fabric manifested in the empowerment of grassroots organizations and the valorization of endogenous resources that participatory processes of sustainable development will take place. Lopes (2006, p. 374) emphasizes that without committed participation in development that aims for autonomy, there is no community animation. For their part, Dias and Palma (2001, p. 42) consider that the multisectoral nature of the intervention makes animation an instrument of local community development (Sánchez Sánchez, 2002, p. 249) and allude to the idea that «(. ..) small-scale animation [community animation] is important when you want to encourage and provoke a process of local development (...)» (Dias & Palma, 2001, p. 45).

The Economic and Social Council (1996, pp. 48-51) in terms of promoting local development potential lists a set of objectives, including job creation; population fixation; promoting the environment and improving quality of life; new support systems for social services, traditional arts and crafts, the promotion of local animation agents and initiatives. The pursuit of the objectives allocated to promoting local development enshrines projects in the areas of social support (free time activities, services aimed at elderly people, among the initiatives, focus on leisure activities, tourism and others), services focused on tourism and leisure (tourist profitability of heritage sites, local tourist circuits, tourist entertainment and information, initiatives in the rural and ecological tourism segment), services oriented towards cultural activities (protection and recovery of historical-cultural heritage, promotion of shows, recreational, sporting and entertainment activities).

The authentic dynamics of community development are based on the participation of local actors and contribute to a model of sustainable development through the use of endogenous assets, through respect and appreciation of the communities' cultural matrix, through the optimization of the user relationship with the resources allocated, through self-development and well-being. - individual and collective social being. Because we observe the didactic principle of participation in community development processes, we highlight one of the different approaches to local development policies: the one centered on «[...] development initiated in the locality and/or region below (participation and mobilization of the community).» (Silva & Silva, 2008, p. 7).

Sociocultural animation as a methodology for community intervention has a preponderant role in enhancing the territory, in boosting endogenous assets, in the social and cultural valorization of communities and is a pedagogy of participation capable of contributing to the promotion of channels of citizen involvement in local development initiatives . It is through sociocultural animation through cultural, educational and socioeconomic dynamics that aim to develop skills and knowledge through permanent learning processes that there is room for the promotion of local democratic governance and social autonomy.

Community development is "the set of processes by which a population joins its efforts with those of public authorities in order to improve its economic, cultural and social situation [...]." (Silva, 1963, p. 7). This multidimensionality of development is shared by Lopes (2016, p. 381) who considers that sustainable local development cannot materialize without a parallel and integrated process, combining technical, economic, cultural and social aspects. Quintana Cabanas (1995, p. 186), Silva e Silva (2008, p. 6), Vásquez Barquero cited by Sánchez Sánchez (2002, pp. 250-251) and the Economic and Social Council (1996) have a similar position when conceptualizing development in the economic, social, cultural, personal and political dimensions.

Development is not restricted to the quantitative phenomenon - «more having», this is accompanied by the qualitative phenomenon - «more being» or «better being» (Silva, 1963, p. 6). This stage of development, from our perspective, points to the principle of community awareness and participation in community development processes due to effective awareness of the surrounding reality, community needs and endogenous potential of the territory, enabling it to sustainable use of community assets.

6. Tourism and the social economy as instruments of sustainable development

6.1. Tourism, a catalyst for community (dis)involvement

Tourism as a sociocultural phenomenon is one of the great human activities of the 21st century and plays a driving role in community development in terms of social, political, economic, cultural, educational, biophysical and aesthetic dimensions (Organización Mundial del Turismo, 1980; ICOMOS, 1999 , p. 2; Rifai, 2017), with repercussions on the sociocultural, environmental and economic sustainability of the host communities.

The valorization and protection of heritage as tourist assets, bearers of history and culture, fragments of community identity, spiritual values and socio-cultural authenticity are aims of community work, when considering tourist development in the non-formal educational and socio-cultural animation dimension (Martins, 2001). This scenario calls for the development of a collective tourist consciousness that prioritizes the principle of safeguarding authenticity, because the satisfaction of tourist needs should not pose a threat to the social and economic interests of indigenous populations, natural resources and historical and cultural places of tourist regions (Organización Mundial del Turismo, 1980, p. 3).

The World Tourism Organization (Mourão, 2000, p. 103) lists a set of principles to be observed by sustainable tourism: understanding and knowledge of the impacts of tourist activity on the natural, cultural and humanized landscapes of the territories; preservation of natural and cultural resources as factors of community well-being; creation of companies providing services added to the tourism sector, consequently generating local employment; promoting the improvement of collective equipment and infrastructure; strengthening local cultural identity and community self-esteem as factors facilitating cultural exchange.

The principle of sustainability evoked in public tourism policies (Decree-Law no. 191/2009, of 17 August) contemplates the valorization of the socio-cultural authenticity of the host communities manifested in material and immaterial heritage, as well as the economic viability of the sector as basis of local and regional economies.

In the context of sustainability - economic profitability, critical mass capable of managing the tradition/innovation binomial, significant cultural offer, infrastructural reception conditions (Marujo & Ramos, 2011, p. 30) - and sociocultural authenticity, it is important to “praise the differentiation» marked by community cultural identity, by the preservation and profitability of cultural assets, by the unique characteristics of the territories and by the exaltation of natural and cultural landscapes.

The contribution of tourism to sustainable development is materialized in five pillars: economic, the structuring foundation of inclusive growth; the social, boosting jobs and empowering communities; the environmental, decisive in the conservation and enrichment of the environment; the cultural, promoting the preservation of diversity, identity and material and immaterial cultures; that of peace, a basic requirement for development and progress (Rifai, 2017).

Tourist activity, respecting the principles of sustainability, is a factor of social balance, generating employment, well-being and empowerment of local communities. Tourism, according to Rifai (2014), is an economic industry supported by people and built on social interaction, as prosperity lies in the integration of indigenous communities and the encouragement of social values: participation, education and improvement of local governance.

ICOMOS (1999) alludes to the idea of cultural and natural heritage, diversities and living cultures being major tourist attractions, along with the need to ensure tourist sustainability and the safeguarding of heritage. This is a plan that involves a group of social and political actors in the definition and management of tourism policies that should prioritize the authenticity of communities and their heritage: maintenance of local vernacular architecture, authentic revitalization of traditions and other heritage particularities.

In contrast to the idea that tourism leads, unilaterally, to cultural and social changes in indigenous communities, consequently, to cultural homogenization, Marujo and Ramos (2011, p. 29) highlight the positive factors of tourist activity: contribution to recovery and (re)invention of traditions, revitalization of community practices, promotion of identity and social cohesion.

In this interpretative line, we highlight the vision of Pereiro Pérez (2003, p. 181) who alludes to the public recognition of the interrelationship between cultural heritage and socioeconomic development. According to this author “You can create development for a cultural event [...], but you can also invent a cultural event to generate development [...].” (Pereiro Pérez, 2013, p. 183) and argues that between tourism and cultural heritage there can be a relationship based on the «Creation of common needs and interests.» (Pereiro Pérez, 2013, p. 183).

Within the scope of tourism policies, one of the areas of activity is the promotion and encouragement of the valorization of heritage as a “tourist environment”. This asset, according to Fernandes (2008, p. 334), is the target of growing national interest in rural-cultural tourism observed as an element of local and regional development and social well-being of local populations. Rural tourism contributes to local development, when understood from a «[...] integral, endogenous and participatory perspective [...].» (Pereiro Pérez, 2013, p. 282).

From our perspective, the tourist industry in the products of cultural tourism and nature tourism, in the form of tourism in rural areas observed within the framework of sustainable tourism, are paradigms of community development (ICOMOS, 1999, p. 7; Mourão, 2000) and, consequently, contributors to improving the quality of life of local populations due to the safeguarding of heritage.

Cultural assets are icons of a set of tourist entertainment activities that contribute to safeguarding heritage, its socio-cultural authenticity and singularities.

Tourist entertainment aims to promote social interactions based on intercultural and multicultural coexistence between tourists and the population of tourist places. An articulated coexistence between the cultural, the educational and the social, seeking to foster a pedagogy of mediated participation in communication, in the living of experiences and in the sharing of knowledge that consolidates human mobility on the path of discovering cultural values.

In our view, the exercise of active citizenship should be extended to tourist activity. Sociocultural animators have the responsibility of fostering creative dynamics and processes, so that the local community can be the protagonist and manager of local initiatives that involve tourists from a social and cultural perspective, with the aim of awakening a sense of discovery, appreciation and appropriation of endogenous assets of the territory and community.

The *Carta Mundial del Turismo Sostenible +20* (Cumbre Mundial de Turismo Sostenible, 2015) focuses on the need to preserve the knowledge held by elderly people regarding natural and cultural heritage through transmission to younger generations, as a means of intergenerational integration of sustainability . This is a principle that promotes social integration of all local actors in tourism development. Tourist entertainment can contribute positively to intergenerationality and, consequently, to intergenerational education projects.

Tourist entertainment is a key element in the community dynamism of the territory. Tourists look for a distinct degree of authenticity of the destination's uniqueness in entertainment activities. The participation of the local population in tourist entertainment activities contributes to the inclusion of the community in tourism dynamics and is a guarantee of the authenticity of the culture, which generates gains in the tourist experience and locals renew their interest in the socio-cultural assets and values of the territory (Alves & Ferreira, 2009). In the opposite scenario, «The lack of entertainment could represent a strong constraint on tourist development [...].» (Vieira, 2005, p. 3).

Heritage assets are integral elements of the culture, history and identity of communities. Within the scope of tourism segments, we observe the existence of a strong support for community cultural assets as resources for the development of sustainable tourism (Council of the European Union, 2014), because «[...] there is no tourist entertainment without conservation of our landscape humanized, [...].” (Barbosa, 2005, p. 7).

It is important that tourism is not alien to the principles of social economy and is in line with the premises of local community development. Safeguarding authenticity and socioeconomic development are areas of intervention that must be managed with and by locals, in an open process of involvement of all actors in tourism policies.

Tourism education and governance must be political programs undertaken boldly in local and regional contexts, involving communities and civil society organizations with (in)direct responsibilities in the tourist territory.

Tourism education is an added value to the community's learning in terms of planning and enjoying the benefits of tourism. It is through education for tourism in formal, non-formal and informal learning contexts that the community will gain tourism awareness as a primary condition for participation in community dynamics for the development of tourism (Rebelo, 1998; Martins, 2001).

6.2. The social economy: valuing the place and social cohesion

In the line of action proposed by UNESCO (1976, p. 7) on the creation of mixed economy structures within the framework of safeguarding and sociocultural dynamization of historical complexes, we contextualize this pair of paradigms within the scope of local community development and as highlighted by Quintana Cabanas (1995 , p. 189), there is an alternative economy that emerges as a response to the social and cultural needs of groups and communities: the social economy.

The alternative economy model (social economy), as a sign of social entrepreneurship, privileges the primacy of people by promoting citizen protagonism, the satisfaction of individual and collective needs through the production of goods and services, without neglecting responses to collective interests through promotion of the common good (Campos, 2005, p. 7; Caeiro, 2008).

The social economy as a space for action and socioeconomic transformation places work at the center of economic and human activities, as a vital element of social inclusion and integration, consequently, a contributing factor to local community development. A *human dimension* is associated with work because people are protagonists of the solidarity economy. There is a *social dimension* because individual capabilities are put at the service of everyone, that is, there is a collective contribution to satisfying the needs of the community. A *political dimension,* in the sense that everyone has full, equal access to social opportunities to acquire resources, the right to work, social dialogue and participation in planning regarding the production of goods and services to satisfy community needs. No less important, an *economic dimension* because it advocates employment and decent working conditions that satisfy people's socioeconomic needs, as well as equitable forms of valuing exchange in commercial and productive relations (Guridi & Pérez de Mendiguren, 2014, p. 35).

The social economy is a socioeconomic space characterized by a set of organizations producing goods or services, social (re)connections (Observatório da Economia Social Portuguesa [OBESP], 2011, p. 2) and «(...) a range of practices that integrate it [the socioeconomic space] solely due to its own nature." (Boyfriend, 2017, p. 1). It is important to consider the social economy as a strategy for socioeconomic inclusion and another model of sustainable development, as everyone involved in self-managed economy organizations are beneficiaries of the economic, social, cultural and political results (Campos, 2005, p. 7; Silva & Silva, 2008, p. 5). In our view, it is fundamental to think of the social economy as a community economy supported by participatory and democratic ethics (Guridi & Pérez Mendiguren, 2014).

The Basic Law of the Social Economy defines this model of community economy as a set of social and economic activities developed freely by cooperatives, mutual associations, charities, foundations (and other private institutions of social solidarity), associations with altruistic activity in the cultural and recreational spheres. , sports and local development, among others, entities falling within the community and self-managed subsectors (cooperative and social sectors).

Social economy organizations operate under a set of principles listed in the Basic Law: the primacy of people and social objectives; free and voluntary membership and participation; democratic control of management bodies; interest in the common good; autonomous and independent management of public entities and private organizations that carry out activities outside the sphere of the self-managed economy; respect for the values of solidarity, equality, equity, subsidiarity, justice, social cohesion, transparency and individual and collective social responsibilities; allocation of surplus to the achievement of the organization's purposes in accordance with the collective interest.

Alternative economy organizations, by promoting citizen protagonism, reinforce social capital in communities, foster social inclusion and cohesion, contribute to community development in economic, ecological, social and cultural matters, giving rise to the use and valorization of endogenous resources in a perspective of integrated and sustainable development (Campos, 2005, p. 7; Caeiro, 2008; Guridi & Pérez de Mendiguren, 2014).

The social economy drives local development dynamics through the valorization of endogenous assets, social and territorial cohesion. There are local development processes when there is the use of endogenous resources, promotion of social and cultural values of the community, production of goods and management of services under the control of local institutions and people, resulting in benefits for them and for the local environment (Silva & Silva, 2008, p. 7).

The *Cascais Charter for the Social Economy* (Conselho Nacional de Economia Social, 2013, p. 1) contains the guiding principle of a model of “stable and sustained development”, promoting the democratization of the economy and responsible consumption, where the primacy of intervention is the valorization of human beings and the development of their skills, based on the protagonism of people and the promotion of local communities. We talk about a social economy that, in the words of Namorado (2017), seeks to be a human economy because it is designed to be at the service of the common good.

From the perspective of Gendron (2004) and according to Guridi and Pérez de Mendiguren (2014, pp. 41-42), it is not possible to talk about sustainable development without considering another economy, as the challenge lies in rethinking the relationship between the economy and the social. Gendron considers that social economy organizations are key actors in sustainable development because they are agents of change and promoters of institutional, social and economic mobilization.

The *new social economy* - the solidarity economy - referred to by Roque Amaro (personal communication, 2005) is the result of the rekindling of the concept of social economy in the early 1980s, which began to have concerns in the fields of defending culture and heritage, the environment, the preservation of rural territories, local development, tourism and local services. Guridi and Pérez de Mendiguren (2014, p. 20) state that the *new social economy* was coined by sociologist Jean-Louis Laville to name companies and organizations in Europe, from the 1970s onwards, as a response to the economic crisis and to the changes taking place in the international economic scenario.

The social economy «[...] increasingly asserts itself as an overlap between the economic and the social, [...]. An overlap that implies systematic interdisciplinarity, [...].” (Boyfriend, 2017, p. 3). It is within the scope of community intervention through social economy projects and/or in the field of sustainable tourism development that sociocultural animators integrated into multidisciplinary teams will be able to contribute to the (de)development of local communities.

Final considerations

Heritage is a source of cultural identity, social cohesion and endogenous resources in the dynamics of local community development. The multiple approaches to heritage assets must materialize based on the observance of different conceptual perspectives that attest to cultural assets as signs of social, environmental, cultural, spiritual and economic wealth.

In the context of cultural governance, sociocultural animators should be facilitators of platforms for active community participation in the definition of policies and the execution of projects that contribute to the preservation and promotion of heritage in its material and immaterial matrix.

The processes of raising community awareness for the exercise of cultural citizenship should provoke community dynamics to safeguard heritage. Cultural assets as a common good imply the involvement of all social actors.

Heritage education as a formal, non-formal and informal educational methodology contributes to creative approaches to transmitting historical-cultural, artistic and educational values. Sociocultural animation as a didactics of participation is a privileged tool in community cultural work.

There are two areas of intervention that enter the local community development formula: tourism and the social economy in a logic of sustainability of communities and their cultural assets. From our perspective, tourism and the social economy are levers for community development. The approach to the principles of sustainable tourist activity and the functional principles of the social economy are matters that sociocultural animators must observe within a broad framework of intervention in the context of local community development. The bases of this development model are the territory, endogenous assets and the community. In the local development process it is vital to consider exogenous development.

Sociocultural animators as development agents are facilitators of the pedagogy of participation and must be committed to the autonomy of groups and the community. Animators have the sociopolitical responsibility of contributing to the creation of spaces for structured dialogue, of (dis)involvement of local actors in the search for solutions to collective problems, of strengthening community contexts for participation in the dynamics and processes of local community development .

Bibliography

Alves, T., & Ferreira, CC (2009). The Lunar Side of Tourist Entertainment: a strategy for tourism and territorial planning and development. In Peres, AN, & Lopes, MS (Coord.), *Tourist Entertainment* (pp. 96-106). Chaves: Portuguese Association of Animation and Pedagogy (APAP).

Assunção, P. (2017). Cultural tourism and heritage education: raising awareness about the importance of preservation. *Unicap History,* 4(7), 15-30.

AA.VV. (2000). *Krakow Charter 2000. Principles for the Conservation and Restoration of Built Heritage.* Accessed on August 22, 2018, at http://www.patrimoniocultural.gov.pt/media/uploads/cc/cartadecracovia2000.pdf

AA.VV. (2016). *Kraków Recommendation for the Protection of Cultural Heritage* . Accessed on August 22, 2018, at http://www.patrimoniocultural.gov.pt/static/data/cartas econvencoes international/tradu caodadeclaracaodecracovia.pdf

Alexandrino, J.M. (2011). The Concept of Cultural Good. In Gomes, CA, & Ramos, JLB (Org.), *Culture and Cultural Heritage Law* (pp. 225-244). Lisbon: Institute of Legal and Political Sciences of the Faculty of Law of Lisbon.

Ander-Egg, E. (1992). *Cultural policies at municipal level.* Argentina: Ediciones CICCUS.

___________ (2003). *Municipal action, local development and community work* . Guía de Isora: Ayuntamiento de Guía de Isora.

Aranha, M.R., & Chaves, L. (2004). Interview with Architect Gonçalo Ribeiro Telles. *People and Places* , pp. 4-5. Accessed on August 17, 2017, at http://www.minhaterra.pt/wst/files/jornalpl16.pdf

Barbosa, A. (2005). Tourist entertainment, development partner. *People and Places* , p. 6. Accessed on September 20, 2018, at http://www.minhaterra.pt/IMG/pdf/jornalpl30.pdf

Caeiro, JMC (2008). Social economy: concepts, foundations and typology, *Katálysis* , 11(1), 61-72.

Campos, MC (2005). Social economy - another way of entrepreneurship. *People and Places* , p. 7. Accessed on August 17, 2017, at http://www.minhaterra.pt/IMG/pdf/jornalpl31.pdf

Chaui, M. (2006). *Cultural citizenship: The right to culture* . São Paulo: Editora Fundação Perseu Abramo.

Coelho, MJP, & Monteiro, LL (1987). *Live History: Cultural Entertainment Proposals using the "Living History" technique.* Lisbon: Portuguese Association of Museology.
European Commission. (2004). *Towards an integrated approach to European cultural heritage.* Accessed on August 2, 2017, at http://eur-lex.europa.eu/legal-content/PT/TXT/PDF/?uri=CELEX:52014DC0477&from=EN

Council of Europe. (1975). *European Charter for Architectural Heritage.* Accessed on August 22, 2018, in http://www.patrimoniocultural.gov.pt/media/uploads/cc/CART AEUROPEIADOPATRIMONI OARQUITECTONICO.pdf

Council of the European Union. (2012). *Council conclusions of 26 November 2012 on cultural governance (2012/C 393/03).* Accessed on August 2, 2017, at http: //eur-lex.europa.eu/legal-content/PT/TXT/?uri=uriserv:OJ.C .2012.393.01.0008.01 .ENG&toc=OJ:C:2012:393:TOC

(2014). *Council Conclusions of 21 May 2014 on cultural heritage as a strategic resource for a sustainable Europe (2014/C 183/08).* Accessed on August 2, 2017, at http://eur-lex.europa.eu/legal- content/PT/ALL/?uri=CELEX%3A52014XG0614%2808%29

__________________(2014a). *Council Conclusions on participatory governance of cultural heritage (2014/C 463/01).* Accessed on August 2, 2017, at http://eur-lex.europa.eu/legal-content/PT/TXT/?uri=CELEX%3A52014XG 1223%2801%29

Economic and Social Council (1996). *Local Development Initiatives.* Lisbon: Economic and Social Council.

National Council for the Social Economy. (2013). *Cascais Charter for the Social Economy.* Accessed on September 10, 2017, at http://www.cases.pt/wp-content/uploads/Carta de Cascais para a Economia Social post CNES.pdf

Cuenca López, J.M. (2014). The role of heritage in educational centers: building heritage socialization, *Tejuelo. Didactics of Language and Literature. Education* , 19(1), 76-95 .

World Sustainable Tourism Summit (2015). *World Sustainable Tourism Charter +20* . Accessed on September 20, 2018, at http://cartamundialdeturismostenible2015.com/wp-content/uploads/2016/05/Carta- Mundial-de-Turismo-Sostenible-20.pdf

Decree no. 49/79 of 6 July. *Official Gazette* No. 130/79 - I Series. Lisbon: Directorate-General for Political Affairs.

Regulatory Decree no. 18/99 of 27 August. *Official Gazette* no. 200/99 - I Series-B. Lisbon: Ministry of the Environment.

Regulatory Decree No. 17/2003 of 10 October. *Official Gazette* No. 235/2003 - I Series-B. Lisbon: Ministry of Cities, Spatial Planning and Environment.

Decree-Law No. 191/2009 of 17 August. *Official Gazette* No. 158/2009 - I Series. Lisbon: Ministry of Economy and Innovation.

Decree-Law No. 149/2015 of August 4th. *Official Gazette* No. 150/2015 - I Series. Lisbon: Presidency of the Council of Ministers.

Dias, N. & Palma, G. (2001). *Giving a Face to the Intervention - Local Development Animators.* Faro: In Loco Association.

Duarte, A. (1994). *Heritage education: guide for teachers, educators, museum monitors and free timers.* Lisbon: Texto Editora.

Fernandes, L. S. (2008). Tourism and local development: the contribution of rural-cultural tourism, *MÁTHESIS,* 17, 333-337.

Florêncio, SRR (2012). Heritage Education: a mediation process. In Tolentino, AB (Org.), *Heritage education: reflections and practices* (pp. 22-29). João Pessoa: Superintendence of Iphan in Paraíba.

European Forum of Those Responsible for Heritage (2009). *Vienna Declaration. An incentive for assets in a period of economic recession* . Accessed on August 22, 2018, in http://www.patrimoniocultural.gov.pt/media/uploads/cc/DECLARACAODEVIENA.pdf

Garrido Arroyo, MC, & Hernández Carretero, AM (2014). Cultural heritage: a participatory management proposal, *Tejuelo. Teaching of language and literature. Education,* 19(1), 62-75.

Grunberg, E., Horta, M.L.P., & Monteiro, A.Q. (1999). *Basic Guide to Heritage Education.* Brasília: National Historical and Artistic Heritage Institute, Imperial Museum.

Guridi, L., & Pérez de Mendiguren, JC (2014). The economic dimension of Local Human Development: The social and solidarity economy. Accessed October 10, 2018, at http://publicaciones.hegoa.ehu.es/uploads/pdfs/265/Economiasocial y solidariaDHL.pdf?1488539833

Hernández Hernández, F. (2002). *Cultural heritage: memory recovered.* Gijón: Ediciones Trea, SL.

ICOMOS (1999). *International Charter for Cultural Tourism* . Accessed on August 18, 2017, in http://www.turismodeportugal.pt/Portugu%C3%AAs/AreasAtividade/desenvolvimentoeinovacao1/Documents/Doc10CartaInternacionalTurismoCultural.pdf

(2011). *La Valletta Principles for the Safeguarding and Management of Historic Cities and Urban Complexes* . Accessed on August 22, 2018, at https://www.icomos.org/images/DOCUMENTS/Charters/VallettaPrinciplesPortugese.pdf

Law no. 13/85 of 6 July. *Official Gazette* no. 153/85 - I Series. Lisbon: Assembly of the Republic.

Law No. 19/2000 of 10 August. *Official Gazette* No. 184/2000 - I Series-A. Lisbon: Assembly of the Republic.

Law no. 107/2001 of 8 September. *Official Gazette* No. 209/2001 - I Series-A. Lisbon: Assembly of the Republic.

Law No. 30/2013 of May 8. *Official Gazette* n. 88/2013 - I Series. Lisbon: Assembly of the Republic.

Law No. 75/2013 of September 12th. *Official Gazette* No. 176/2013 - I Series. Lisbon: Assembly of the Republic.

Law No. 50/2018 of August 16th. *Official Gazette* No. 157/2018 - I Series. Lisbon: Assembly of the Republic.

Leitão, LMT (2011). The Enjoyment of Cultural Goods. In Gomes, CA, & Ramos, JLB (Org.), *Culture and Cultural Heritage Law* (pp. 319-333). Lisbon: Institute of Legal and Political Sciences of the Faculty of Law of Lisbon.

Lopes, MS (2006). *Sociocultural animation in Portugal.* Keys: Intervention.

Lopes, MS (2014). Tourist Entertainment: Concepts, foundations, objectives and paradigms. In Lopes, MS, Maltez, MA, & Pereira, JDL (Coord.), *Sociocultural Animation: Tourism, Heritage, Culture and Local Development* (pp. 63-73). Keys: Intervention.

López de Aguileta, I. (2000). *Culture and city. Municipal cultural policy manual.* Gijón: Ediciones Trea, SL.

Lourenço, F., & Moreira, J.M. (2014). The Logic of Governance - Governance - in Public Tourism Policies, *Revista Gestão & Políticas Públicas* , 4(1), 22-44.

Marujo, MN, & Ramos, FM (2011). Socio-Anthropological Reflections on Tourism, *Revista Turismo & Desenvolvimento* , 16, 25-33.

Martins, EC (2001). One of the challenges of the millennium: education for tourism, *Aprendir,* 30, 105-110.

Martín González, M.T., & Quiroz Nino, C. (2000). Development and Participation. In Martín González, MT (Coord.), *Economía Socialy Animación Sociocultural* (pp. 37-89). Madrid: Sanz y Torres.

Miranda, J. (2011). Notes on Culture, Constitution and Cultural Rights. In Gomes, CA, & Ramos, JLB (Org.), *Culture and Cultural Heritage Law* (pp.159-181). Lisbon: Institute of Legal and Political Sciences of the Faculty of Law of Lisbon.

Mourão, JM (2000). *Sustainable Tourism Development - principles, fundamentals and practice. Geolnova,* 2, 87-117.

Boyfriend, R. (2017). What is the Social Economy? *Social Economy in Texts,* 1. Coimbra: Center for Cooperative and Social Economy Studies.

Portuguese Social Economy Observatory (2011). *The Social Economy: Concept proposed by OBESP.* Accessed on November 7, 2018, at https://www.cases.pt/wp-content/uploads/OBESPConceito de Econom iasocial 09DEC 2011.pdf

Order of Economists - Madeira Regional Delegation (2012). *VI Annual Tourism Conference - Conclusions and recommendations.* Accessed on October 30, 2018, at https://www.economistasmadeira.org/images/documentos/eventos/ConclusoeRecomnedacoesVICAT.pdf

World Tourism Organization (1980). *Manila Declaration on World Tourism.* Accessed October 30, 2018, at https://www.e-unwto.org/doi/pdf/10.18111/unwtodeclarations.1980.6.6.1

(1982). *Acapulco Document.* Accessed October 30, 2018, at https://www.e-unwto.org/doi/pdf/10.18111/unwtodeclarations.1982.8.6.1

(1995). *Sustainable Tourism Charter. Accessed on October 30* , 2018, at https://www.e-unwto.org/doi/pdf/10.18111/unwtodeclarations.1995.21.15.1

Pereiro Pérez, X. (2013). *Cultural Tourism. An anthropological view.* Maia: ISMAI and CEDTUR Editions.

Pinto, H. (2014). *Challenges of Heritage Education: teaching and learning history in heritage sites* . Accessed on August 5, 2017, at http://clio.rediris.es/n40/articulos/mono/MonPinto2014.pdf

Quintana, J. (1993). *The professional areas of Animation* . Madrid: Narcea Ediciones.

Quintana Cabanas, J.M. (1995). Precisions on local development, *Social Pedagogy. Revista Interuniversitaria* , 10, 185-191.

Rebelo, SM (1998). Municipal Tourism Education Plan - PMET: a model for Brazilian municipalities with tourism potential, *Turismo - Visão e Ação,* 1(2), 89-103.

Resolution of the Assembly of the Republic no. 47/2008 of 18 July. *Official Gazette* No. 177/2008 - I Series. Lisbon: Assembly of the Republic.

Resolution of the Council of Ministers no. 96/2000 of 7 July. *Official Gazette* No. 171/2000 - I Series-B. Lisbon: Presidency of the Council of Ministers.

Rifai, T. (2014). *Message from the Secretary General of the OMT Taleb Rifai.* Accessed on October 30, 2018, at http://wtd.unwto.org/es/content/unwto-secretary-generalwtd2014

(2017). *Sustainable tourism as a development instrument.* Accessed on October 30, 2018, in http://cf.cdn.unwto.org/sites/all/files/sg official messagewtd2017 s.pdf

Sánchez Alonso, M. (2000). Sociocultural Animation and Social Economy. In Martin González, MT (Coord.), *Economia Social y Animación Sociocultural* (pp. 1-36). Madrid: Sanz y Torres.

Sánchez Sánchez, R. (2002). Sociocultural animation and local development, *Anales: Anuario dei Centro de la UNED Calatayud,* 1(10), 247-263.

Santos, PM (2005). Interview with Rogério Roque Amaro. *People and Places,* pp. 4-5. Accessed on August 17, 2017, at http://www.minhaterra.pt/IMG/pdf/jornalpl31 .p df

Serrano, R. (2007). The legacy of generations in the construction of the landscape. *People and Places,* p. 8. Accessed on August 17, 2017, in http://www.minhaterra.pt/wst/fil es/Jornal PL45.pdf

Silva, MM (1963). *Bases of a Community Development process.* Accessed on January 30, 2017, at http://www.repository.utl.pt/bitstream/10400.5/1402/1/MS-AS- 1963-2.pdf

Silva, AS (1994). What is integrated development? A reflection, with empirical illustration. In Associação Portuguesa de Sociologia (Ed.), *Cultural Dynamics, Citizenship and Local Development* (pp. 591-619). Lisbon: Portuguese Sociology Association.

Silva, JLA & Silva, SIR (2008). *The solidarity economy as the basis of local development.* Accessed on August 15, 2017, at https://eces.revues.org/1451

Singer, P. (2002). *Introduction to the Solidarity Economy.* São Paulo: Editora Fundação Perseu Abramo.

UNESCO (1976). *Recommendation on the safeguarding of historical sites and their role in contemporary life.* Accessed on August 30, 2017, at http://www.patrimoniocultural.gov.pt/media/uploads/cc/salvaguardaconjuntoshistoricos1976.pdf

(1976a). *Recommendation regarding the participation and contribution of popular masses in cultural life* . Accessed on August 22, 2018, at http://unesdoc.unesco.org/images/0011/001140/114038s.pdf#page=146

(2003). *Convention for the safeguarding of intangible cultural heritage* . Accessed on August 25, 2017, at https://ich.unesco.org/doc/src/00009-PT-Portugal- PDF.pdf

Ventosa Pérez, V. (2009). Tourist Entertainment and Sociocultural Entertainment: relationships and differences. In Peres, AN, & Lopes, MS (Coord.), *Tourist Entertainment* (pp. 146-151). Chaves: Portuguese Association of Animation and Pedagogy (APAP).

Vieira, C. (2005). The role of tourist entertainment in rural territories. *People and Places* , p. 3. Accessed on September 20, 2018, at http://www.minhaterra.pt/IMG/pdf/jornalpl30.pdf

MIX
Papier aus verantwortungsvollen Quellen
Paper from responsible sources
FSC® C105338

FSC
www.fsc.org

Printed by Books on Demand GmbH, Norderstedt / Germany